# THE LONDON PANORAMAS
## OF
# ROBERT BARKER AND THOMAS GIRTIN

*circa* 1800

Hubert J. Pragnell

London Topographical Society
*(Hon. Editor: Marjorie B. Honeybourne)*
No. 109

1968

© Hubert J. Pragnell, 1968

Publication no. 109 of the
London Topographical Society
50 Grove Lane, London S.E.5

PRINTED IN GREAT BRITAIN BY HEADLEY BROTHERS LTD
109 KINGSWAY LONDON WC2 AND ASHFORD KENT

# Contents

# List of plates

# Acknowledgements

This monograph owes much to Mr. John Priestley and Miss M. B. Honeybourne (L.T.S. Editor) for their constant encouragement and help; Mr. E. Croft-Murray (Keeper of Prints and Drawings at the British Museum); Mr. J. T. Hayes (Assistant Keeper of the London Museum); Mr. D. Jolly (Assistant Keeper of the Whitworth Gallery, Manchester); Mr. C. S. Minto (City of Edinburgh Librarian); Mr. J. Gage (Lecturer in Fine Art in the University of Norwich); Mr. Levinson-Lessing (Keeper of European Painting at the Hermitage Museum, Leningrad); Mr. T. Girtin; Mr. P. Jackson; Mr. F. Kelsall and Mr. P. Snelgrove.

Thanks are also due to the Courtauld Institute of Art, the Greater London Council Records Department, the Guildhall Library, Southwark Borough Library and Messrs. Sotherby and Co.

The following have kindly allowed reproduction of prints and drawings: the Trustees of the British Museum (Plates I–VII, IX–XII, XIV, XVI), the Guildhall Library (Plate VIII), the Trustees of the London Museum (Plate XIII), the Greater London Council (Plate XV) and Professor J. Isaacs (Plate XVII).

# I. *Panoramic painting*

London has inspired many panoramic artists since the days of Wyngaerde, the sixteenth-century pioneer. In the next century Visscher and Hollar also depicted London prior to the Great Fire of 1666. With the greater interest in topographical art in the eighteenth century, London, with its skyline of Wren's dome, towers and spires, became a favourite subject. Many examples of such work survive but two of the more unusual are lost. These are Robert Barker's 'Panorama of London', painted in 1790–1791, and Thomas Girtin's 'Eidometropolis or Panorama of London', probably dating from 1800-1801.

Interior decoration conveying the illusion of space beyond the walls of a chamber can be traced back to ancient Egypt, to a painting of *c.* 1370 B.C., with the illusion of papyrus groves, in the Northern Palace at El Amarneh. Wall-painting continuing the architectural ornament of the interior into the landscape beyond was a common feature of Italian palaces during the Renaissance, perhaps the most famous being the view of Rome seen through colonnades in the Villa Farnesina, painted by the architect Baldassare Peruzzi between 1508 and 1511. The earliest surviving example of this kind of painting in England is at Eastbury Manor, Barking, and dates from the first half of the seventeenth century. The first identified artist of this kind of mural decoration was George Portman, 'scenographer' at the court of Charles I, who painted eight of 'The Queenes Majesties Houses in Landskipp' on the walls of Oatlands Palace. A hundred years later Canaletto, who had been painting the Venice of his day, was invited through his acquaintance with the British Consul to come to London in *c.* 1745. His panoramas from Somerset House and Lambeth are world-famous. Probably a little later Paul Sandby (1730–1809) painted for Drakelow Hall, Derbyshire, a large view of 'Peak' scenery, part of which is now in the Victoria and Albert Museum. J. L. Roget in his *History of the Old Water-Colour Society* mentions George Barret, a native of Dublin and a founder-member of the Royal Academy, as a pioneer of panoramic painting. Barret with others painted a continuous view of Cumberland lakeland scenery on the walls of a large room at Norbury Park, near Dorking, the home of Rev. John Locke. The figures and statues were the work of Cipriani, Sawrey Gilpin painted the cattle and Bernedetto Pastorini the sky. Sir George Beaumont (1753–1827), Constable's patron, has also been claimed as a pioneer: for his 'circular room' Thomas Hearne planned a 'View of the Lake and Vale of Keswick from Crow Park'; but this was never executed. Meantime realism was taken a stage further in 1781 by Philip de Louthenburg, a native of Strasbourg who had settled in London. He exhibited a moving panorama called the 'Eidophuoikon' in which changing lights suggested changes in the time of day and the weather. There were two scenes, 'View of London from Greenwich Park' and 'Port of Tangier', in which the rising moon contrasted with a fire in the Mediterranean. Gainsborough was so influenced by this scenic effect that he painted a miniature 'Eidophuoikon' of his own on glass slides.

So far all panoramas had been drawn or painted on a flat surface. The next development was in the late 1780's by Robert Barker, who is said to have been the first to paint on a cylindrical surface. He had conceived the idea whilst sketching on Calton Hill, Edinburgh. Born in Kells in 1739, Barker had tried without much success to establish himself in Irish artistic circles before settling as a portrait painter in Edinburgh. After making a special study of perspective he carried sketches of his new type of pictorial representation to London and showed them to Sir Joshua Reynolds, who pronounced any semi-circular panorama impractical but added that he would leave his bed at any time in the night to inspect such a work. Barker duly set to work on his first panorama, 'Edinburgh from Calton Hill',[1] a full-circle view which he exhibited in Edinburgh and Glasgow (where his son, Henry Aston, was born, 1774) before showing it in London at 28 Haymarket. Barker may have been encouraged in this venture by Lord Elcho, son of the Earl of Wemyss. According to an advertisement of March, 1789, Barker's Edinburgh view 'affords the spectator a complete prospect of the whole horizon as appearing from the top of the observatory on Calton Hill comprehending a circle of several hundred miles. The idea of this view is perfectly original and pleasing.' Sir Joshua, who was living nearby at 47 Leicester Square, congratulated Barker, whose next panoramic work was 'London from Albion Mills, Southwark', exhibited in the capital from the beginning of 1792.

Other artists were soon attracted to panoramic painting,[2] with varying degrees of success. One such artist was Robert Ker Porter, whose panorama, 'The Storming of Seringapatam, 1799', attracted considerable attention when exhibited at the Lyceum in 1800. It was 120 feet long, semi-circular, and is said to have been painted in six weeks. Porter produced further panoramic views which, judging from the frequency of new titles, also met with success. Porter was acquainted with Thomas Girtin and may well have encouraged him in this direction, although his main inspiration must have been Barker's view of London. For example, the viewpoints of both Barker's and Girtin's panoramas were only a few yards apart. Barker chose the roof of the Albion Mills at the south-east end of Blackfriars Bridge on ground now occupied by the railway. Girtin selected the roof of the terraced houses on the west side of Albion Place abutting on the British Plate Glass Manufactory. Previous writers have assumed that Girtin took his view from the actual roof of this manufactory but this statement seems to be incorrect unless the terraced houses were the property of the glass company, which seems most probable.[3] Plate XV is a view from the Thames of the British Plate Glass Manufactory drawn in about 1800, which shows how the terrace overshadowed the roof of the factory. Plate XVII, a sketch of the south prospect for Girtin's panorama, shows the perspective recession of the terrace roof with the foreground of Albion Place obscured in consequence. The 'View of London from Blackfriars Bridge' by N. R. Black (Plate XIII) was also taken from the terraced houses in Albion

Place, probably from a second-floor window, judging from the elevation of the upper windows of the mills.

In the nineteenth century, panoramas of London were still popular, though much smaller than Girtin's huge townscape. The Crace Collection at the British Museum contains engravings of panoramic views of London by William Daniels (*c.* 1805) and others, as well as J. Henshall's circular view from the cross of St. Paul's Cathedral, painted in 1836. Panoramic painting continued well into the nineteenth century. Favourite subjects were views of European capitals, beauty spots, the Himalayan mountains, ports in the Far East painted from the sketches of travellers, naval and military campaigns and victories. Henry Aston Barker, who had watched his father develop the idea of panoramic views, was one of the keenest exponents of this artistic trend.[4] His eldest brother, Thomas Edward Barker, also took up panoramic painting, in partnership with John Burford, who regularly exhibited panoramas at his own Panorama building at 169 Strand (converted in 1831 into the Strand Theatre).[5] The above-mentioned Robert Ker Porter exhibited several panoramas besides his 'Storming of Seringapatam' at the Lyceum in the Strand. The titles included 'The Siege of Acre, 1800', 'The Battle of Agincourt, 1801', 'The Battle of Alexandria, 1801', 'The Battle of Lodi, 1803', and 'The Defeat of the French, Mont St. Gothard, 1804'. Porter later gave up painting for foreign travel and made extensive tours of Persia, Armenia and Russia, where he died in 1842. James de Maria, another artist attracted to this type of painting, exhibited a 'Grand Panorama of Paris and Environs'[6] in the Haymarket, next door to the Opera House, during the spring and summer of 1802, just after Girtin's return from France. John Reinagle also produced several panoramas in the early years of the nineteenth century. Two further buildings, the Colosseum and Vauxhall Gardens, were then displaying panoramic work. The former, a circular building in Regent's Park, was built in 1824 to display Thomas Horner's view of London from St. Paul's—'a stupendous painting occupying a surface of 46,000 feet'. At Vauxhall these pictorial attractions were variously known as panoramas, dioramas and cosmosramas, and some had additional attractions such as special lighting effects. Almost as grand as the spectacles were the titles: the one painted by F. Thorne and exhibited at Vauxhall in 1823 was 'Bay of Naples by Moonlight, and a vivid representation of Mount Vesuvius in a state of active Combustion'. Panoramas continued to attract and entertain until their decline in the 1850's, hastened by the development of photography.

## II. *Barker's Panorama of London*

Robert Barker's Panorama of London only survives in the form of six aquatints, a set of which are in the Crace Collection[7] at the British Museum. Preliminary sketches for the panorama were made by Barker's son Henry Aston, prior to March 1791, when the Albion

Mills were burnt out.[8] From the sketches the son made engravings, which were converted into aquatints by Frederick Birnie. These are on six sheets, each measuring 22 inches by 17 inches, and were published simultaneously with the exhibition of the Panorama at 28 Castle Street, in 1792. This Panorama was a very popular attraction throughout that year. *The Times* of 10 January carried the following announcement:

PANORAMA

The public are most respectfully informed that the subject at present of the PANORAMA painted by R. Barker, Patentee for the invention, is a view at a glance of the CITIES of LONDON and WESTMINSTER, comprehending the three bridges, representing in one Painting, containing 1479 square feet, which appears as large and in every respect the same as reality. The observers of this Picture being by painting only deceived as to suppose themselves on the Albion Mills, from which the view was taken.

The PANORAMA is open for inspection from NINE o'clock every Morning, till FOUR in the Afternoon.

Admittance One shilling.

No. 28, Castle Street, Leicester Square.

The announcement was repeated in the London press periodically throughout 1792 but from 1 January 1793, came a change:

The public are respectfully informed that the Painting of the PANORAMA of LONDON and WESTMINSTER will be lighted up with lamps which have a beautiful effect, and will open for inspection every Monday and Thursday Evening from six till nine.

This Panorama of London, painted in distemper on canvas, was first exhibited as a semi-circular work. The full circle, suggested by Barker's mother, was subsequently completed after the opening of Barker's new premises in Leicester Square, to which the panorama was transferred before the close of 1793. Barker's first exhibition in Leicester Square was announced as follows in *The Times* of 5 September 1793:

Barker's new Panorama of Spithead [at the] Panorama, Leicester Square, by Royal Patent, present subject contains 10000 square feet and is a view of the Grand Fleet moored at Spithead being the Russian armament.

The Panorama at No. 28, Castle Street, is a View of London and Westminster.

Barker moved his exhibition from Castle Street (demolished in the Charing Cross Road redevelopment of the 1880's) because with the rising popularity of the panoramic form of art larger premises were needed for satisfactory display. With the aid of a public subscription Barker built the Panorama in Leicester Square expressly for the exhibition of panoramas. The building was designed by Robert Mitchell of Newman Street and was situated between Leicester Place and Cranbourne Street. It contained three circular rooms, the largest 90 feet in diameter and 40 feet in height, for the display of full-circle works to be viewed from a distance of 30 feet. Barker's 'Spithead' was a full-circle oil panorama. This became the talk of the town and was visited by George III and Queen Charlotte.

For the painting of these enormous panoramas Robert Barker erected a large circular wooden building near 14 West Square, St. George's Fields, his home from 1799 to 1806.[9] A wash drawing, 9 in. by 5 in., by J. Buckler of this 'Building for painting the Panoramas near West Square, Southwark' is in the Guildhall Library (Plate VIII).[10] West Square is south of Blackfriars Road and St. George's Circus.

On Robert Barker's death in 1806 the building called the Panorama in Leicester Square passed to his second son, the above-mentioned Henry Aston Barker, who in 1802 had married a daughter of William Bligh, Commander of the *Bounty*, and lived at 13 West Square from 1802 to 1824. On Henry's retirement the Panorama building was given to his brother's partner, John Burford and his son Robert, who managed it until the former died in 1861. Owing to the decline in interest in panoramic works the Panorama was then closed and the building later became a penny news-room. The site is now occupied by the French Church of Nôtre Dame. The building is not named on Horwood's large-scale plan of London, 1792–1799, but the second edition, published in 1807, shows a rectangular building bounded on the west by Leicester Place, north by Lisle Street, east by Portaville Passage and south by Cranbourne Street. This was the approximate position of Barker's building.

Barker's panorama is particularly valuable as showing south London in detail, especially the vista down Surrey Street, which in Girtin's work is known only by a simple pen drawing scaled for transfer (Plate XVII). Blackfriars Bridge, however, makes the best starting point for a survey of Barker's London Panorama. This bridge was the third London bridge to be built. It was designed by Robert Mylne, opened in 1769 and replaced between 1865 and 1869 by Thomas Cubitt's present iron bridge. At the north end of the bridge is shown Chatham Place leading into New Bridge Street, with Fleet Market beyond (Plate I).

The next section (Plate II) eastward shows the city skyline dominated by St. Paul's Cathedral. It is hard without actually seeing Barker's panorama to judge the accuracy of its draughtsmanship but this aquatint by F. Birnie would suggest that Barker's panorama was inferior to the views of Girtin and Black. On the other hand an aquatint must to a certain extent formalize the picture and destroy the atmospheric illusion created by oil, water-colour or distemper. The river shows a variety of light craft including in the left foreground a barge flying the standard of the Royal Exchange Fire Office. A correspondent in *Notes and Queries* in 1851 said that he remembered seeing Barker's Panorama in Castle Street and that it included the water procession on Lord Mayor's Day. However, from the number of trees in full-leaf the work would suggest a summer scene, not 9 November, the traditional date for the Lord Mayor's Show.

St. Paul's Cathedral has defied the accuracy of artists ever since its completion and Henry Aston Barker seems to have been no exception. His rendering of the dome is poor whilst the proportions of the stages of the western towers are inaccurate. This section of the panorama is useful, however, as a record of the many church towers and spires, although again the draughtsmanship is poor. The most prominent churches on the west side of St. Paul's are St. Sepulchre, Holborn; St. Martin, Ludgate, with a small dome; and Christchurch, Newgate Street, with St. Andrew-by-the-Wardrobe just in front. To the east of St. Paul's is the spire of St. Augustine, Watling Street, an oriental onion shape. This spire was the one designed for the church by Wren in 1695–1697. It was altered in 1830–1831, but after severe damage during the air-raids of 1940 the tower and spire have been restored to their original late seventeenth-century appearance.[11]

Barker's viewpoint from the Albion Mills has the advantage over Girtin's of showing the eastern part of the city as well as Southwark, and the forest of masts in the Pool below London Bridge (Plate III). Girtin's view directly to the east was blocked by the Albion Mills, which must have been one of the tallest buildings on the south bank. The windmill[12] to the right of centre was on the roof of Skelton's Meeting House in Maiden Lane after that building had been converted into a warehouse and post mill for grinding bones in the late 1780's. The tower beyond the windmill is that of St. Saviour's, Southwark, now the cathedral. It was here that Thomas Girtin was baptised in 1775.[13] The eastern horizon is dominated by Shooters Hill.

The next section (Plate IV) although largely an area of roof gives a good impression of the suburban development creeping across south London, but the townsman still had no further to go than Camberwell and Peckham to reach open fields. The two furnaces on the left belonged to the Falcon Coal Wharf, and the spire beyond is that of St. George the Martyr, Southwark.

The full circle is completed by the view south-west across Albion Place and down the street shortly afterwards to be re-named Blackfriars Road (Plates V and VI). This thoroughfare had been laid out in 1765[14] as the southern approach to Blackfriars Bridge from St. George's Circus, and on Horwood's map is named Great Surrey Street from the Circus to its junction with Albion Street and Stamford Street just beyond the pediment of the roof (Plate V). Albion Place had the façade of the Albion Mills running the entire length of its east side, as seen in Girtin's water-colour sketch (Plate XVI). On Edward Moggs's map of 1804 the whole thoroughfare from St. George's Circus to Blackfriars Bridge is named Blackfriars Road, but Stockdale's map of 1817 retains the original name. According to H. B. Wheatley (in *London Past and Present*) the road was known as Great Surrey Street until about 1829.

A further advantage of Barker's panorama over that of Girtin is the wealth of detail shown in the Georgian terraces in Albion Street and Albion Place. These terraces were built at intervals from about 1780. Several still remain on the east side though distorted by modern shop fronts. The rest had been demolished by the end of the nineteenth century. On the corner of the terrace on the west side of Albion Street stood the Cross Keys Coffee House with its sign fixed to the corner above the first-floor windows. The adjoining house in Albion Street has an elaborate portico. The clean architectural lines of the terraced houses on the west side of Albion Place are shown to advantage in Plate V with the Thames curving towards Westminster in the far distance. Here, with no obstructing building behind, can be seen Girtin's viewpoint. Also, there are instances of everyday street life, such as men carrying out road repairs at the approach to the bridge, and a man carrying a sack on his back. At the first front door in Albion Place someone awaits an answer from within whilst a woman looks down from a first-floor window.[15] The name 'Albion Place' can be distinctly seen incised in the stone stringcourse, then the fashionable form of street identification.

It is a great pity that Barker's panorama itself has vanished. It most likely ceased to be displayed at the Panorama in Leicester Square after the summer of 1794 as Barker's next panoramic work, the 'Glorious First of June, 1794', was ready for exhibition. Robert Barker died on 8 April 1806, at 14 West Square, and was buried in St. Mary's Church, Lambeth. His son, Henry Aston Barker, continued the family tradition for another twenty years. In fact, in 1802 he had already exhibited in London a panorama of Paris.[16] It is possible that his visit to Paris in that year may have influenced Girtin to go there too, for shortly before his untimely death he was himself contemplating a large view of the French capital. One hint can be put forward as to further showings of Barker's London panorama. William Whitley, writing on Girtin's panorama of London in the *Connoisseur* for May 1924, mentions a panorama of London exhibited on the continent at the beginning of the nineteenth century; and when this panorama was displayed in Vienna in 1801 it was described as 'after the English fashion' and showing London from the Albion Mills.[17] This, then, would seem to be Barker's work. Descriptive plans of it were prepared in French and Dutch, and one of the French copies is among the Prints and Drawings in the British Museum (Plate VII).

# III. *Thomas Girtin's 'Eidometropolis' or Panorama of London*

This panorama also has vanished. Until recently it was only known from five water-colour sketches and one ink-and-wash drawing in the British Museum,[18] though a descendant of the artist, also named Thomas Girtin, owns two pen-and-ink studies for the work.[19] Another pen-and-ink drawing, scaled for transfer (Plate XVII) was sold at Sotheby's on 22 December 1965, as Lot 122, described as 'School of Thomas Girtin'. This sketch is the only known record of the view to the south, and Mr. Croft-Murray sees no reason to doubt its authenticity as it bears all the characteristics of a Girtin drawing. Until its discovery Girtin's panorama was assumed to have been semi-circular because of an inaccurate etching by Louis Francia, published in 1803, which condensed the section showing south London.[20]

The exact date of execution of Girtin's panorama is generally thought to have been between 1800 and 1802, although the artist's failing health has inclined several writers to favour 1797–1798, the date of the sketches. In the *Library of the Fine Arts*, volume III (1832), it is claimed that the panorama was completed by Girtin 'aged 23 years'. He was born in

1775. In spite of poor health throughout his life his output was prodigious, especially during his last few years. He made frequent sketching tours throughout the length and breadth of England as well as seizing the opportunity afforded by the Treaty of Amiens for a hurried visit to Paris between November 1801 and May 1802. Lawrence Binyon (*The English Water-Colour Painters*) felt that Girtin's vast output might have hastened his death. His panorama was probably finished before he left for France as he was then contemplating a panoramic view of the French capital and made sketches for that purpose. During the few months remaining to Girtin after his return to London he produced some of his finest water-colours as well as a number of etchings of Paris. He was still at work in his room, over Norman's carving and gilding shop at 441 Strand, when he died of asthma or consumption on 9 November 1802. He was buried in the churchyard of St. Paul's, Covent Garden, and the mourners included Turner, Beechey and Hearne.

Some difference of opinion has been expressed over the medium used by Girtin for his panorama but it is generally accepted that it was in oils. Girtin's obituary notice in the *Morning Herald* of 12 November 1802 is quite specific:

> His Panorama of London exhibited at Spring Gardens will serve, though
> only his second attempt in oils, as a monument to perpetuate his fame.

Girtin's other oil painting was of Bolton Bridge, Yorkshire.

Girtin's 'Eidometropolis or Panorama of London' was exhibited in the Great Room, Spring Gardens,[21] from 2 August 1802, after the showing of Samuel James Arnold's 'Panorama of the Battle of Alexandria'. Girtin probably painted his huge work at J. S. Hayward's floor-cloth manufactory at 37 Newington Causeway, Southwark, for Hayward was his assistant.[22] The first press announcement of this new panorama was in the *Morning Post and Gazetteer* for Monday, 2 August:

> T. Girtin most respectfully begs leave to inform his friends and the public in
> general that his GREAT PICTURE OF LONDON 108 feet long and 18 feet high,
> taken from the top of the British Plate Glass Manufactory near Blackfriars Bridge,
> comprehending London and its environs will if Mr. Girtin's health permits, be
> open for exhibition This day, August 2, at Mr. Wigley's Great Room, Spring
> Gardens.

The exhibition was open from 9 a.m. until dusk and admission was 1s. Further short announcements appeared in the London newspapers at frequent intervals. *The Times* of 25 August carried this slightly longer notice:

> Eidometropolis, a great picture of London, Westminster and its environs now
> exhibiting at the Great Room, Spring Gardens.   Admission 1s.   T. Girtin returns
> his most grateful thanks to a generous public for the encouragement given to
> his exhibition, and as it has been conceived to be merely a picture framed, he
> further begs leave to request the notice that it is a Panorama, and from its magni-
> tude which contains 1944 square feet, gives every object the appearance of being
> the size of nature. The situation is so close as to show to the greatest advantage the
> Thames, Somerset House, Temple Gardens, all the churches, bridges, principal

buildings, etc. with the surrounding country to the remotest distance, interspersed with a variety of objects characteristic of this great Metropolis. His views of Paris, etched by himself, are in great forwardness, and to be seen with the picture above.

Another reference to the London panorama, in the *Morning Post and Gazetteer*, 22 October 1802, records that 'T.G. flatters himself that the subject will be found highly interesting with the wonderful array of buildings and towers as well as the elegance of Blackfriars Bridge'.

Girtin's 'Panorama of London' was well received by the *Monthly Magazine and British Register, Monthly Retrospect of the Arts*. In September 1802, it proclaimed 'Mr. Girtin's EIDOMETROPOLIS or great circular picture of London, Westminster and environs to be upon a scale two feet longer than Mr. Porter's "Storming of Seringapatam".' The issue for October 1802 included this very favourable review of Girtin's masterpiece:

> Mr. Girtin's Eidometropolis at Spring Gardens is very well attended, and, considered in all its points, may fairly be placed in the very first class in this new and extraordinary appropriation of perspective to painting. The artist, it seems, did not take the common way of measuring and reducing the objects, but trusted to his eye, and has by this means given a most picturesque display of the objects that he has thus brought into his great circle; and, added to this he has generally paid particular attention to representing objects of the hues which they appear in nature, and by that means greatly heightened the illusion. For example, the view towards the east appears through a sort of misty medium arising from the fires of the forges, manufactures, etc. which gradually lessen as we survey the western extremity.
>
> Blackfriars Bridge is a prominent object, and St. Paul's rises with the most majestic dignity above all the surrounding buildings. Though the Temple Gardens and some other parts are of a much lighter tint than the general masses, the whole is in harmony, and the eye is not hurt by spots. The water is pellucid and, contrary to what we have seen in pictures of this description, varies in colour; that near the shore very properly partaking of the hue of the earth beneath. The craft upon the river is boldly and forcibly relieved; the figures in Blackfriars Road, where there is a ring surrounding two pugilists, are correctly represented, and the horses, asses, etc. have very great spirit.
>
> The apparent space which the objects seem to occupy, and their relative size, give them the appearance of being much larger than they really are. The person who attends the visitors measured one of the figures, which proved to be only four inches high; and to determine a dispute whether some earthen chimney-pots that were on one of the houses were three or four feet long, did the same by them, and they proved to be no more than six inches. The front of the Albion Mill would have been better if it had been more kept down in colour, and Westminster Bridge we suspect to be more circular than it is in nature. The two towers of Westminster Abbey appear in one mass, which destroys that lightness and air which constitutes a leading beauty in the building. From the point of view from which it is taken it is probably a true representation, but a licence is allowed to painters as well as to poets; and where a picturesque effect can be produced, a trifling deviation would, in a picture of this description, be overlooked or forgiven. On the whole, we consider it the connoisseur's panorama, and hope the young and very meritorious artist will obtain the approbation to which he is so justly entitled.

17

The reference to the eastern prospect appearing through mist would seem to indicate that the final version, the panorama, differed from the sketches as the greatest concentration of industry appears in the latter in the western foreground (Plate X). Also, no pugilists appear in the sketches showing the approach to Blackfriars Bridge.[23]

Girtin's sketches afford a fascinating glimpse of late eighteenth-century London. The water-colour of Westminster and Lambeth (Plate IX), $20\frac{3}{4}$ in. by $11\frac{5}{8}$ in., creates a wonderful illusion of distance with the heights of Clapham on the horizon. In the foreground are the tiled roofs of the houses in Upper Ground, with several rows of terraced houses beyond in Stamford Street. The windmills[12] on the left or western horizon were near Newington Butts. Further to the right or east is silhouetted the tower of St. Mary's, Lambeth, with the louvre of Lambeth Palace rising above a group of trees. Further to the right again on the north bank of the Thames are the towers of St. John's Church, Smith Square, built by Thomas Archer. Nearby is the roof of Westminster Hall, and behind is Westminster Abbey, both dominating the skyline as they were to continue to do until the rebuilding of the Houses of Parliament after the fire of 1834. In spite of the small size of these sketches Girtin's water-colour technique is outstandingly superior to the younger Barker's aquatints in conveying general atmosphere, distance, smoke and mist.

Girtin's next water-colour (Plate X), $21\frac{1}{4}$ in. by $9\frac{5}{8}$ in., shows the sweep of the Thames between Adelphi Terrace and Somerset House. The river was much wider then than today because there was no embankment. The foreground of the picture shows the intensive growth of industry on the south bank in a most dramatic way with the chimneys of James Lukin's Iron Foundry in Upper Ground belching forth black smoke. Beyond is the tower of Watt's Shot Manufactory,[24] described by Samuel Ireland in 1791 as a new structure. Close to the south bank sailing barges ride at anchor off Bull Stairs and Nicholson's Timber Yard. The sweep of the north bank is treated with great delicacy and shows Girtin's intense love of London's architecture as well as his mastery of water-colour. It was to 8 Adelphi Terrace, the home of Dr. Monro, that Girtin, Turner and many other young artists came to sketch and seek advice, and were given 'oisters and half-crowns', so every street, court and alley in this neighbourhood must have been known to Girtin. To the right of Watt's shot tower but on the north bank is the octagonal pyramid-shaped wooden water-tower of the York Buildings Waterworks Company, probably erected in the 1690's. The Company supplied water as far as Piccadilly, Whitehall and Covent Garden, and this tower, about seventy feet in height, appears in several views by Samuel Scott and Canaletto. The spire in the far distance is that of St. James's, Piccadilly, and St. Martin-in-the-Fields rises beyond Adelphi Terrace. Chambers's masterpiece of Somerset House, the home of the Royal Academy between 1780 and 1837, dominates the Thames-side buildings then rising from the water's edge. The tower and spire of St. Mary-le-Strand, its Portland stone glistening in the sun, appear above the rooftops.

The next view to the east (Plate XI), 19 in. by $8\frac{3}{4}$ in., shows the Thames from the Temple to Blackfriars, with the tower of St. Clement Danes prominent to the west. The Inner Temple buildings and King's Bench Walk are easily distinguished behind Temple

Stairs. Eastward are timber wharves and Whitefriars Dock. Nearby was Bridewell, where according to tradition Girtin was imprisoned for a short time for refusing to finish his apprenticeship to Edward Dayes, the water-colourist and engraver. In the distance appears the tower of St. Andrew, Holborn. This picture must be seen in colour fully to appreciate Girtin's wonderful rendering of London's smoke-laden and misty atmosphere.

Unfortunately, no water-colour sketch by Girtin survives for Blackfriars Bridge and St. Paul's; and in the British Museum's working drawing in ink and grey wash (Plate XII), 20¾ in. by 14 in., the sky is damaged by marks of oil and distemper. However, there is in the London Museum a large water-colour of London painted by Nathaniel R. Black (Plate XIII). It is from almost the same viewpoint as Girtin's panorama and gives a clear representation of this section of the view. Black, who seems to be a virtually unknown artist, exhibited at the Royal Academy between 1798 and 1803, and painted two views of London from this position. The water-colour in question, probably painted from a second-floor window of one of the terraced houses opposite Albion Mills, was exhibited in 1798 and described in the Royal Academy catalogue as No. 399, 'View of London from Albion Place'.[25] The figures were added by J. C. Barrow. Black's other picture, 'View of London from the Surrey side of Blackfriars Bridge', was shown at the Academy in 1801. It is pure conjecture whether Black was influenced by Barker's panorama or Girtin's sketches. Black's finished picture was probably made from sketches made prior to March, 1791, as the façade of the Albion Mills on the extreme right of the picture is shown intact, not derelict as a result of the fire of that date. Black continued his view further south than Girtin and shows the south end of Blackfriars Bridge, where the parapets make a graceful gradually-widening outward curve. A note on this water-colour is at the British Museum among the papers of W. T. Whitley: he mentions a large coloured engraving of Nathaniel Black's view of London, dated 2 May 1802, and displayed in Ackerman's window in Bond Street on 8 July 1924. This engraving, apparently very accurate but wholly inartistic, was by J. C. Stadler.

In Girtin's sketch many city landmarks are recognizable although the prominence of St. Paul's, beautifully drawn, is slightly exaggerated. The spire on the extreme left or west is that of St. Bride's, Fleet Street. In the far distance, beyond the northern approach to Blackfriars Bridge, are the towers of St. Sepulchre, without Newgate; St. Martin, Ludgate; and Christchurch, Newgate Street. Added depth is given to the sketch by the tinted warehouses near St. Paul's. By the entrance to Puddle Dock are anchored several sailing barges.

The most dramatic of Girtin's water-colour sketches is the one of the Thames from Queenhithe to London Bridge with threatening storm clouds overhead (Plate XIV), 17½ in. by 8⅞ in. Most of the church towers can readily be identified though many have long since disappeared (Plate XVIII). On the extreme east is the Tower of London. The brick façades of the riverside warehouses are treated very delicately with yellow-ochre washes, and their stone-courses are suggested by leaving the white surface of the paper untinted.

In his next water-colour sketch (Plate XVI), $21\frac{1}{4}$ in. by $12\frac{15}{16}$ in., a large part of Southwark lies hidden behind the derelict Albion Mills, rather light in tone and somewhat clean for a burnt-out building. The mills were designed by Samuel Wyatt and John Rennie for grinding flour on a large scale by Watt's steam engines and were virtually the first attempt to rotate millstones by the application of steam power. When opened in 1786 the mills met with considerable opposition as millers claimed that the new mechanical process for grinding corn would create unemployment and eventual starvation; and also that the Albion Mills Company would have the monopoly of corn-milling in London and so would be able to charge a high price. The Company on the other hand were quick to point out that the public would benefit by increased production and that the mills would not be affected by stoppages due to frost, floods and droughts as in the case of watermills, and lack of wind for wind-mills. The Company did not foresee that the mills during their short life would encounter labour difficulties and trouble with the engines. The mill owners were not mechanics and had often to seek the aid of Boulton and Watt at their Soho factory in Birmingham. The fire which destroyed the mills broke out at 6 a.m. on 2 March 1791, and reduced the interior to ruins in only two hours. The cause of the fire was never established but incendiarism was suspected. Another theory was that the fire was due to the great friction of the eight millstones. The walls remained standing well into the nineteenth century and for a time formed the front of a row of private houses. All trace of the Albion Mills disappeared with the construction of a goods station and depot for the London, Chatham and Dover Railway in the 1860's. Part of the site was, according to Wilkinson's Survey of Christchurch Parish, 1821, occupied in his day by Quincey's Timber Yard.[26] The foreground of Girtin's picture is Albion Place, drawn faintly in pencil. At the corner of Albion Street is a Georgian bow-fronted shop, fashionable then in London. Above the parapet of the Albion Mills to the east is the tower of St. Saviour's, Southwark, while to the right of the mills is St. George-the-Martyr, Southwark.

The last section, completing the full circle, is the newly-found pen-and-ink drawing already mentioned (Plate XVII), $19\frac{3}{4}$ in. by 11 in. The terraced houses in Great Surrey Street, built shortly after the thoroughfare had been laid out, are sketched without detail. In the middle distance is the roof of Rowland Hill's Surrey Chapel, built in 1786 and later to become 'The Ring', of boxing fame, bombed in 1941. The tower of Christchurch, Southwark, rises prominently on the right or east of the sketch. The body of this church was destroyed in 1941 and has subsequently been rebuilt to a modern design. The Rotunda in front of the church tower was built in 1788–1789 to house Sir Ashton Lever's Museum of Natural History and Antiquities. It later became the Surrey Institution and was not finally demolished until the early 1950's. It was behind 3 Blackfriars Road. In the drawing some of the roofs of the houses are marked with the word 'slate', a material then coming into use for roofing.

Unfortunately Louis Francia's very inaccurate etching[20] of Girtin's panorama was published on 29 January 1803, less than three months after Girtin's death. This etching condensed the southern section so completely that it appears as if it were part of the south bank immediately west of the British Plate Glass Manufactory, where Lukin's Iron Foundry should stand. Also, the Albion Mills façade is cut into two so as to appear at both ends of Francia's semi-circle as two separate buildings. Why Francia should have drawn such a distorted version is hard to explain as he must have been able to consult the actual panorama if not the sketches as well. Perhaps the drawing was done in haste to commemorate Girtin. Whatever the cause Francia, despite contemporary descriptions, created a false impression of Girtin's 'Eidometropolis' for over a century.

With Girtin's untimely death the gallery in Spring Gardens closed but a few days after his burial it was re-opened for the benefit of his widow and son. What eventually happened to the panorama is unknown although Henry Bates Dudley, writing in the *Morning Herald* in December 1802, made certain suggestions for its future. He wrote:

> The recent death of that extraordinary and celebrated artist, Mr. Thomas Girtin, may be considered as a national loss. The Eidometropolis exhibited at Spring Gardens, both in magnitude and effect, stands unrivalled. We advise our readers not to lose the opportunity of seeing it before it closes, which will be on the last day of this month, when we believe it will come under the hammer. In viewing this magnificent concern the connoisseur stands enraptured, and feels an emulation in protecting genius; and every Briton and lover of his country also, in seeing his native place, the glory of the world, so finely and truly portrayed.
>
> The accuracy of Mr. Girtin's eye was such that every house was attended to; all the churches, bridges, the Thames, etc. with the numerous craft, Blackfriars Bridge and the Surrey Road; and embellished with the astonishing variety of objects that characterizes this great commercial city. It might be fitted up to form an elegant object in a nobleman's or gentleman's park; it would be novel, and would furnish its owner with an opportunity of seeing London though in the country, and would be fortunately gratifying to his visitors from the endless variety it contains. The antiquary in a few years would see what London was, and mark the great alterations that are about to take place, particularly at London Bridge. It has often been pointed out to the Government the want of a National repository of the Arts, similar to the Louvre in France; this, we think, would make a proper object, and might be worthy their attention. Before we take our leave, we request our friends to take notice of the smoke floating across the picture from Lukin's Foundry, the impending storm over the City, and the grandeur of St. Paul's.

These ideas did not materialize. Instead the panorama is said to have lain rolled up for many years in a loft over a carpenter's or architect's shop in St. Martin's Lane, and in about 1825 was sold by E. Cohen, second husband of Girtin's widow, to a Russian nobleman who took it to St. Petersburg. There is no further trace of it.[27]

Had Girtin's life not been so short he might well have attained the artistic fame of his contemporary and close friend, William Turner. As it was Girtin placed the art of water-colour painting on a new level of importance and was one of the finest exponents of this branch of English art. In regard to panoramic art, the *Gentleman's Magazine* in February 1803, specially praised Girtin's London panorama, which 'may if taken in all its points be fairly considered as the most classic picture that has yet been taken in that branch of art, which may fairly be denominated the triumph of perspective'. Girtin's Panorama of London undoubtedly excelled all others for a further reason. Girtin had the eye and feeling of a Londoner. Born in Southwark he grew up to know and love every brick and stone in his environment, so that he was inspired to paint London as if his very life was built around the trials and fortunes of the city.

# Notes

1 An engraving by J. Wells of Barker's Edinburgh panorama is in the Huntley House Museum, Edinburgh. Another panorama of Edinburgh was painted by John and Robert Burford and exhibited at the Panorama in Leicester Square in 1825.

2 On 23 May 1803, Constable wrote as follows to his friend, John Dunthorne:

> 'Panoramic painting seems to be all the rage. There are four or five now exhibiting and Mr. Reinagle is coming out with another, a view of Rome, which I have seen. I should think he has taken his view favourably, and it is executed with the greatest care and fidelity.'

For a general account of panoramic painting, especially as a form of interior architectural 'trompe l'oeil' decoration, see E. Croft-Murray's forthcoming book.

3 James Elmes in his *Topographical Dictionary of London* (1831), definitely says that the terraced houses on the west side of Albion Place belonged to the British Plate Glass Manufactory.

4 Henry Aston Barker's (1774–1856) last panorama was exhibited in 1823 and depicted the Coronation Procession of George IV. He died near Bristol (obituary in *The Gentleman's Magazine*, 1856, 515–518). See also *Art Journal*, 1857, 46.

5 The British Museum has a six-volume catalogue of the panoramas of Barker and Burford produced between *c.* 1800 and 1850 at the Panorama in Leicester Square and in the Strand. No further panorama of London on such a scale as Barker's and Girtin's seems to have been shown.

6 This panorama was taken from the north-west tower of Nôtre Dame.

7 Portfolio III, 92.

8 See below.

9 Survey of London, XXV, *St. George's Fields* (1955), 64.

10 See (*ibid.*), plate 44b.

11 St. Paul's Cathedral Library, MS. WE 20 (*re* Wren's steeple); Guildhall Library, MS. 8881 (St. Augustine's Repairs Committee Minute Book, 1830–1831), MS. 8917 (Agreement *re* repairs). See also *The Gentleman's Magazine*, September 1831, 218, for an acid comment on the alteration. Mr. R. H. Harrison has kindly supplied this information.

12 K. G. Farries and B. M. T. Marsh, *The Windmills of Surrey and Inner London* (1966), 204.

13 The Register of St. Saviour's, Southwark, records the baptism on 17 March 1775, of 'Thomas, son of John Girtin, brushmaker, and Rose Hannah'.

14 For the lay-out, see J. Summerson, *Georgian London* (1946), 262. Nos. 179–189, Blackfriars Road, are still basically Georgian. Wilkinson's Plan of the Parish of Christchurch, Southwark, 1821, is reproduced in the Survey of London, XXII, *Bankside*, plate 66.

15 A correspondent in *Notes and Queries*, 1851, says that as a boy he saw this panorama: 'I was struck with the baker knocking at the door in Albion Place and wondering the man did not move.'

16 H. A. Barker's sketches for this panorama of Paris are in the Victoria and Albert Museum.

17 *The Monthly Magazine*, 1801, 342.

18 A water-colour, *c.* 1798–1800, in the Whitworth Gallery, University of Manchester (MWI., no.130), thought by T. S. R. Boase to be a Girtin sketch for his London panorama is, after all, not such. The painting shows the southern end of London Bridge, the tower of St. Saviour's and a water tower. It may be by Girtin's friend, John Henderson.

19 These two studies are of Lambeth to Westminster, and the Albion Mills façade.

20 Reproduction in *The Connoisseur*, May 1924; and see below.

21 See Survey of London, XX, *Trafalgar Square and Neighbourhood* (1940), 67. The Great Room was built as a Huguenot chapel in 1716 but was drastically altered by David Cock, the sub-lessee from 1757. For the next fifty years it was a fashionable 'rendezvous' for concerts and exhibitions, including those of the Incorporated Society of Artists from 1761 to 1772. In 1780 Charles Wigley bought the lease and conducted many auctions there. The room measured 62 ft. by 52 ft. In 1827 Decimus Burton built 10, 12 and 14 Spring Gardens on the site. *Kent's London Directory*, 1802, names Wigley and Bishop, music-sellers, and Charles Wigley, jeweller, at 6 Spring Gardens.

22 J. S. Hayward was an amateur landscape painter exhibiting topographical views of England, Wales and Italy regularly at the Royal Academy between 1798 and 1816 (A. P. Oppé in *The Connoisseur*, December 1923, 189–198). In April 1802, Girtin wrote to his brother John from Paris to ask if J. S. Hayward was contemplating a panorama of Paris (letter quoted by W. T. Whitley in *The Connoisseur*, May 1924, 14).

23 In the circular copy of Barker's London panorama (Plate VII) a ring surrounding two pugilists is shown in Albion Place, in front of the Albion Mills. This ring is not on the aquatint (Plate V) as here the pediment of the Albion Mills obscures this part of the thoroughfare. Girtin may have taken the idea of these street pugilists from Barker's work, which he must have known.

24 This shot tower, erected in 1789, suffered in a fire on 5 January 1826. It was used for a time for advertising purposes and was not pulled down until 1937. Its height was 140 feet and the lead fell 123 feet. A second shot tower, 196 feet tall, on the west side of Waterloo Bridge, was built in 1826 and survived until April 1962. It had been used for the manufacture of lead shot until 1949. Constable made sketches from Whitehall Stairs of the opening of Waterloo Bridge in 1817. His last painting of this subject, in 1832, shows both shot towers somewhat inaccurately on the extreme right of the canvas (reproduction in A. Shirley, *John Constable, R.A.*, plate 132).

25 In 1798 Nathaniel Black was living in Bennet Street but by 1801 he was at 1 Albion Place (R.A. Catalogue). Here also lived Alexander Black—almost certainly a relative of his—who was Secretary of the British Plate Glass Manufactory (*Kelly's London Directory, 1795–1801*). He most probably allowed both Girtin and Black to use his premises for their painting.

26 O. A. Westworth in *Economic History*, January 1932, 380–395.

27 The possibility of Girtin's London panorama having been exhibited in St. Petersburg has been discussed with the Keeper of European Painting at the Hermitage, Leningrad. He knows of no such panorama being exhibited in the city in the early nineteenth century and suggested that the 'Russian nobleman' might have been a mistake for Girtin's contemporary and fellow panorama painter, Robert Ker Porter, who collected 'objets d'art' and travelled extensively in Russia. Porter may have commented on the fate of Girtin's panorama but his writings in the British Museum were destroyed in the 1939–1945 war.

# Bibliography

*Notes and Queries*, 24 May–August 1851: correspondence on the origins of circular panoramic art (some confusion and inaccuracies)

Roget, J. L., *History of the Old Water-Colour Society*, 1891

*Art Journal*, 1857, 46–47: Origins of panoramic painting

Croft-Murray, E., *English Decorative Painting, 1537–1837*, II, ch. 6, 'The Panorama Room' (in the press)

Hardie, M., *Water-Colour Painting in Britain*, 1967

Graves, A., *Royal Academy of Arts Dictionary of Contributors, 1769–1904*, 1905

Whitley, W. T., 'Thomas Girtin's Panorama of London' in *The Connoisseur*, May 1924

Mayne, J., *Thomas Girtin*, 1949

Girtin, T., and Loshak, D., *The Art of Thomas Girtin*, 1954

*The Whitley Papers: Notes on Artists* (British Museum, Dept. of Prints and Drawings)

Westworth, O. A., 'The Albion Steam Flour Mills' in *Economic History*, January 1932, 380–395

Taylor, T., *Leicester Square: Its Associations and Worthies*, 1874

Horwood, R., Plan of London, Westminster, Southwark and the Parts adjoining, showing every House, on a scale of 26 in. to 1 mile (reproduced by the London Topographical Society, 1966)

# Index

*Plates*

PLATE I

I. Blackfriars Bridge, view across the Thames to the north bank showing the Temple and St. Bride's Church (aquatint after Henry Aston Barker)

PLATE II

II. The City with St. Paul's Cathedral (aquatint after Henry Aston Barker)

PLATE III

III. View east across the roof of the Albion Mills showing the eastern part of the City,
London Bridge and Southwark (aquatint after Henry Aston Barker)

PLATE IV

IV. South-east London from the Albion Mills, with Sydenham hills on the horizon
(aquatint after Henry Aston Barker)

PLATE V

V. Albion Street, looking south across St. George's Circus
(aquatint after Henry Aston Barker)

PLATE VI

VI. Albion Place, with Adelphi Terrace and Somerset House in the distance
(aquatint after Henry Aston Barker)

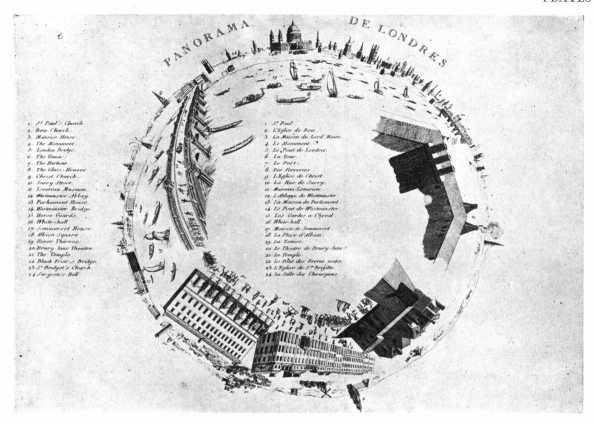

VII. Plan, with English and French wording, of Barker's London Panorama, from a Continental guide to the Panorama (B.M. Dept. of Prints and Drawings)

VIII. Building for painting the Panoramas (of R. Barker and son) near West Square, Southwark (wash-drawing by J. Buckler)

IX. Westminster and Lambeth (water-colour by Thomas Girtin)

X. The Thames from Westminster to Somerset House (water-colour by Thomas Girtin)

XI. The Thames from the Temple to Blackfriars (water-colour by Thomas Girtin)

XII. Blackfriars Bridge and St. Paul's (pen-and-wash drawing by Thomas Girtin)

PLATE XIII

XIII. Blackfriars Bridge and St. Paul's (water-colour by Nathaniel Black)

XIV. The Thames from Queenhithe to London Bridge (water-colour by Thomas Girtin)

XV. The British Plate Glass Manufactory, *c.* 1800 (water-colour, anonymous)

XVI. The Albion Mills (water-colour by Thomas Girtin)

XVII. Great Surrey Street and Christchurch, Southwark (pen-and-ink, most probably by
Thomas Girtin)

PLATE XVIII

1. St. Bride
2. St. Sepulchre
3. St. Martin Ludgate
4. Christchurch, Newgate Street
5. St. Andrew-by-the-Wardrobe
6. St. Paul's Cathedral
7. St. Augustine, Watling Street
8. St. Benet, Paul's Wharf
9. St. Lawrence Jewry
10. St. Mary Magdalen, Old Fish Street (destroyed, 1886)

11. St. Mary-le-Bow
12. St. Nicholas Cole Abbey
13. St. Mildred, Bread Street
14. St. Mary Aldermary
15. St. Mary Somerset
16. St. Michael, Queenhithe (destroyed, 1876)
17. St. Michael, Cornhill
18. St. James Garlickhythe
19. St. Michael Paternoster Royal
20. St. Swithin, London Stone

21. St. Margaret, Lothbury
22. St. Mary Abchurch
23. St. Clement, Eastcheap
24. St. Margaret Pattens
25. The Monument
26. St. Dunstan-in-the-East
27. St. Magnus the Martyr

A. Puddle Dock
B. Paul's Wharf
C. Queenhithe

XVIII. Line-drawing identifying the City churches